5-Minute Bible Studies

Written and Edited by
Thomas J. Doyle and Roger Sonnenberg

Editorial Assistant: Phoebe W. Wellman

Your comments and suggestions concerning this material are solicited. Please write to Product Manager, Youth and Adult Bible Studies, Concordia Publishing House, 3556 S. Jefferson Avenue, St. Louis, MO 63118-3968.

Scripture quotations are taken from the HOLY BIBLE: NEW INTERNATIONAL VERSION ®. Copyright © 1973, 1978, 1984 by the International Bible Society. Used by permission of Zondervan Publishing House. All rights reserved.

The "NIV" and "New International Version" trademarks are registered in the United States Patent and Trademark Office by the International Bible Society. Use of either trademark requires the permission of the International Bible Society.

Copyright © 1994 Concordia Publishing House
3558 South Jefferson Avenue, St. Louis, MO 63118-3968
Manufactured in the United States of America

All rights reserved. Except for the Study Pages, which the purchaser may reproduce for parish programs, no part of this publication may be reproduced, stored in a retrieval system, or transmitted, in any form or by any means, electronic, mechanical, photocopying, recording or otherwise, without the prior written permission of Concordia Publishing House.

3 4 5 6 7 8 9 10   03 02 01 00 99

Contents

"Gotta Minute?" *(Introduction)*

The Promise Keeper *(2 Chronicles 7:14)*	Study **1**
Angels Watching over Me *(Psalm 91:11)*	Study **2**
Who's in Charge? *(Matthew 6:26)*	Study **3**
More Than a Glimmer of Hope *(Romans 8:32)*	Study **4**
His Purpose—My Purpose *(Philippians 1:21)*	Study **5**
Wherever You Go *(Joshua 1:9)*	Study **6**
My Heart Yearns *(Job 19:25–27)*	Study **7**
A "Soft Pillow" of Assurance *(Romans 8:28)*	Study **8**
Neither Height Nor Depth *(Romans 8:38–39)*	Study **9**
Love Is... *(1 Corinthians 13:4)*	Study **10**
Love as He Loves *(1 Corinthians 13:7)*	Study **11**
A Lopsided Exchange *(2 Corinthians 5:21)*	Study **12**
Transformed *(Galatians 2:20)*	Study **13**
His Wound=Our Joy *(Isaiah 53:4–5)*	Study **14**
Resuscitated by Christ *(Ephesians 2:8–9)*	Study **15**
Christ's Attitude *(Philippians 2:5–8)*	Study **16**
Rejoice! *(Philippians 4:6–7)*	Study **17**
I Can with Christ *(Philippians 4:13)*	Study **18**
He's Coming Again *(1 Thessalonians 4:13–18)*	Study **19**
With Confidence *(Hebrews 4:16)*	Study **20**
Faith Is... *(Hebrews 11:1)*	Study **21**
More Than Words *(James 2:14–17)*	Study **22**
A Glimpse into Our Future *(1 John 3:1–2)*	Study **23**
What Will It Be Like? *(Revelation 21:4)*	Study **24**
It Turned Out Okay *(Genesis 50:19–20)*	Study **25**
Walking with God *(Genesis 5:24)*	Study **26**
Falling Back in Love *(Revelation 2:4–5)*	Study **27**

Will Life Ever Get Better? *(Psalm 30:5)*	Study 28
Jesus' Great "Not!" *(Psalm 23:1–6)*	Study 29
Our Refuge and Strength *(Psalm 46:1–2)*	Study 30
A Lamp and a Light *(Psalm 119:105)*	Study 31
What's Your Grade? *(Proverbs 3:5–6)*	Study 32
Jesus Swallowed Death *(Isaiah 25:8–9)*	Study 33
Do You Not Know?!? *(Isaiah 40:28–31)*	Study 34
Drowning in... *(Isaiah 41:10)*	Study 35
Purchased Back *(Isaiah 43:1)*	Study 36
Talking to a Wall *(Isaiah 55:10–11)*	Study 37
Good News *(Isaiah 61:1–3)*	Study 38
Forgive and Forget *(Jeremiah 31:34)*	Study 39
Feet Like a Deer *(Habbakuk 3:19)*	Study 40
What's First? *(Matthew 6:33)*	Study 41
Forgetting the Obvious *(Matthew 7:7)*	Study 42
Built on the Rock *(Matthew 7:24–25)*	Study 43
In a Nutshell *(John 3:16)*	Study 44
If Death Would Only Die... *(John 11:25)*	Study 45
Vine, Branches, and Fruit *(John 15:5–7)*	Study 46
Two Big Words *(Romans 3:23–24)*	Study 47
United We Stand, Divided We Fall *(Romans 6:3–5)*	Study 48
Wages and Gifts *(Romans 6:23)*	Study 49
Do Good to All *(Galatians 6:10)*	Study 50
A Greater Inheritance *(1 Peter 1:3–5)*	Study 51
God's Insurance Policy *(Revelation 2:10)*	Study 52

"Gotta Minute?"

If you are like most people in this fast-paced world your answer to this question is an out-of-breath, "No! I'm kind of in a hurry," "Well…", or "I've got one minute!" Unfortunately, our busy schedules have often hampered or even eliminated communication between husband and wife, parent and child, among co-workers, friends, and possibly most alarming, and between people and God. Weakened or destroyed relationships result. For communication is the cornerstone of healthy and growing relationships.

Because of time limitations and other commitments, many adults fail to receive the faith-strengthening power God promises to provide when His Word is studied—"so is My Word that goes out from My mouth: It will not return to Me empty, but will accomplish what I desire and achieve the purpose for which I sent it" **(Isaiah 55:11).** In discussing the question, "How can I improve Bible study attendance in my congregation?" many exclaim, "I don't know what to do? I've tried just about everything!" Rather than "throwing in the towel," one concerned lay person recently said, "If they won't come to Bible study, than bring the Bible study to them." But how?

"Gotta minute? How about five minutes?" Use the five-minute Bible studies provided in this book. Simply, make copies of one of the Bible studies and distribute it to those attending a meeting, a program, or some other congregational function. There is no need to provide Bibles, because God's Word is printed in each of the Bible studies. Or insert a copy of one of the five-minute Bible studies in your Sunday bulletin. Suggest that worshipers use the five-minute Bible study for home study, private devotions, or family devotions.

Although interest and discussion may turn a five-minute Bible study into a 10- or 15-minute Bible study, the time will be well spent. You will provide participants a time for God to communicate with them through His Word, while also encouraging communication among the participants. The Holy Spirit promises to work through God's Word to strengthen our relationship with Him as we build our relationship with one another.

"Gotta Minute? How about Five Minutes?"

Follow these simple steps to provide a faith-strengthening and relationship-building experience for the people in your congregation.

1. Select one of the 52 five-minute Bible studies.
2. Reproduce a Bible study so that everyone has his or her own copy.
3. Distribute a copy of the Bible study to each participant.
4. If you have a large group, consider dividing it into small groups of three to five participants. This will give everyone an opportunity to share.
5. Read aloud or have a volunteer read aloud the Bible passage.
6. Discuss briefly the questions that follow. *Remember:* All participants should have equal opportunity to share their thoughts and insights.
7. Close the Bible study with prayer using the prayer models or suggestions.
8. Encourage participants to keep their study and use it in their personal or family devotions. Or encourage participants to give the Bible study to a family member, friend, co-worker, etc.

The Promise Keeper
2 Chronicles 7:14

GOD'S WORD

If My people, who are called by My name, will humble themselves and pray and seek My face and turn from their wicked ways, then will I hear from heaven and will forgive their sin and will heal their land. (2 Chronicles 7:14)

FOR SHARING

1. Historians say that the majority of major civilizations have lasted approximately 200 years.
   - From bondage to spiritual faith.
   - From spiritual faith to great courage.
   - From great courage to freedom.
   - From freedom to abundance.
   - From abundance to selfishness.
   - From selfishness to complacency.
   - From complacency to apathy.
   - From apathy to dependence.
   - And from dependence back again to bondage.

   In other words, most major civilizations were not destroyed by enemies from the outside, but by the deterioration from within.

2. What evidence is there that such deterioration is taking place within our country? within our own community? within the church?

3. There's a wonderful promise attached to the warning in the passage. Repeat the promise to the person sitting next to you.

4. The Old Testament Promisekeeper is the Promisekeeper of the New Testament. What promise did He make to us? He arranged to keep the promise through the sacrificial death of His Son Jesus Christ. Now this promise is ours: "If we confess our sins, He is faithful and just and will forgive us our sins and purify us from all unrighteousness" **(1 John 1:9).** Turn to the person next to you and repeat this promise to one another.

PRAYER

Heavenly Father, Promise Maker and Keeper, give us:
   Clear sight to see our sins;
   Humility to confess them;
   Resolution to turn away from them.
Through Jesus Christ. Amen.

Study 1

© 1994 CPH   Scripture references:NIV.

Angels Watching over Me

Psalm 91:11

GOD'S WORD

For He will command His angels concerning you to guard you in all your ways. (Psalm 91:11)

FOR SHARING

1. The psalmist repeats an oft-forgotten truth; angels minister to us. Throughout Scripture we read about angels who serve God's people, fight Satan, protect individuals, guard, announce work from God, guide, translate (accompany God's elect to heaven), worship God, praise God (with voices and instruments), gather resurrected people, and assist Christ in judging the world.

With pen in hand underline the truths about angels of which you were unaware.

2. If each of us has guardian angels watching over us, why does harm sometimes come upon us?

3. How do the life, death, and resurrection of Jesus protect us from the greatest harm—death—the ultimate consequence of sin?

PRAYER

Take a few moments to consider things to pray about
  Almighty God,
  We confess…
  We praise You for…
  And we ask for…
Be with us now. Give us wisdom and guidance in all that we do. In Jesus' name we pray. Amen.

Study 2

© 1994 CPH   Scripture references: NIV.

Who's in Charge?

Matthew 6:26

GOD'S WORD

"Look at the birds of the air; they do not sow or reap or store away in barns, and yet your heavenly Father feeds them. Are you not much more valuable than they?" (Matthew 6:26)

FOR SHARING

1. Someone once said, "Of all the living creatures in our world, only humans accumulate problems and wear them like a yoke around their necks." Respond to this statement.

2. What does God's care of the birds teach us?

3. Jesus never forgot who was in charge. Even as He faced dying on the cross in order to rescue people from sin, death, and the power of the devil, Jesus looked to God. What special concerns do you face now, personally or as a church? Are you looking to God for help? If so, of what can you be assured?

PRAYER

O God, we come to You
    grateful for...
    confessing...
    trusting that...
Through Jesus Christ our Lord. Amen.

Study 3

More Than a Glimmer of Hope

Romans 8:32

GOD'S WORD

He who did not spare His own Son, but gave Him up for us all—how will He not also, along with Him, graciously give us all things? (Romans 8:32)

FOR SHARING

1. An Austrian psychiatrist, Viktor Frankl, while a prisoner in Hitler's concentration camps, witnessed repeatedly the truth that man could survive almost anything, as long as he had a glimmer of hope.

The Christian has more than a hope that is "wishful thinking." He has hope that is an assurance God is in control. God provides for His people. Describe that hope. When has that hope been evident in your lives?

2. If God gave His Son to die for us, why do we not believe that He would also give us everything that we need? Would God go to such lengths only to abandon us when troubles come our way?

3. Knowing the promise of **Romans 8:32,** of what does God assure us as we meet together?

PRAYER

O God, we have come to You
  to thank You for the promise of **Romans 8:32;**
  to ask Your forgiveness for…
  to receive Your guidance for…
For Jesus' sake. Amen.

Study 4

© 1994 CPH   Scripture references: NIV.

His Purpose—My Purpose

Philippians 1:21

GOD'S WORD

For to me, to live is Christ and to die is gain. (Philippians 1:21)

FOR SHARING

1. Paul was in prison when he wrote these words. His friends had deserted him. His health was bad. Death was imminent. And yet, what assurance did Paul have?

2. Complete the phrase: "For me to live is _____." Be honest. What's first and of primary importance in your life? What about in your church? In what way does your answer determine how you look at life?

3. What was Jesus' primary purpose for coming to earth? See **Romans 5:6–8.** How did His purpose give us purpose?

PRAYER

Lord Jesus, give us the joy that comes from knowing that though we may not always live for You, You always live for us. Come, be with us now as we…Guide us. Make us wise so that we might live in You; through Jesus Christ our Lord. Amen.

Study 5

Wherever You Go

Joshua 1:9

GOD'S WORD

"Have I not commanded you? Be strong and courageous. Do not be terrified; do not be discouraged, for the Lord your God will be with you wherever you go." (Joshua 1:9)

FOR SHARING

1. Everyone becomes frightened or discouraged at times. Share with a partner a recent event or situation that frightened or discouraged you? Why were you terrified? discouraged?

2. Often people become terrified and/or discouraged when
   - something occurs to change their well-made plans.
   - a situation is out of their control.

   What promise does God provide us in this passage?

3. Sin causes us to doubt God's promise. How can doubt affect our response to a situation or an event?

4. Thanks be to God! We may doubt or question God's presence and working in our lives, but through Jesus' death on the cross and resurrection from the grave we have forgiveness. He not only forgives us, but He helps us trust Him through His precious Word. How could memorizing the last phrase, "the Lord your God will be with you wherever you go," help you when you begin to feel terrified or discouraged?

PRAYER

Confess to God your doubts that cause you to become terrified or discouraged.
Give thanks to God for His full and complete forgiveness through Jesus' death on the cross.
Praise God for His promise to "be with you wherever you go."

Study 6

© 1994 CPH   Scripture references: NIV.

My Heart Yearns

Job 19:25–27

GOD'S WORD

"I know that my Redeemer lives, and that in the end He will stand upon the earth. And after my skin has been destroyed, yet in my flesh I will see God; I myself will see Him with my own eyes—I, and not another. How my heart yearns within me!" (Job 19:25–27)

FOR SHARING

1. For what does your heart yearn? *Note:* Our hearts usually yearn for the things that complete the sentence: "If I only…then I'd be happy."

2. How do you think most people in society would complete this sentence: "And after my skin has been destroyed"…?

3. How can that for which our hearts yearn, affect that which will occur after "my skin has been destroyed"?

4. Throughout history people have been buried with that for which their heart yearned—Elvis with his car, an elderly woman with her pet cat, etc. These people have challenged the "You can't take it with you" philosophy. Job also challenged this philosophy. How?

5. Through faith in Jesus, God forgives us when our heart yearns for things other than Him. Through His Word He strengthens our faith enabling us to "take it with us" so that we can confess with Job, "And after my skin has been destroyed, yet in my flesh I will see God." Because Jesus lives, of what can we also be assured?

PRAYER

Confess your yearning for things other than God.
Give thanks to God for His forgiveness through Jesus.
Ask God to help you share your confidence and hope in eternal life with others, especially those who do not know Jesus or their Savior.
Praise God for the gift of eternal life through Jesus.

Study 7

© 1994 CPH   Scripture references:NIV.

A "Soft Pillow" of Assurance

Romans 8:28

GOD'S WORD

And we know that in all things God works for the good of those who love Him, who have been called according to His purpose. (Romans 8:28)

FOR SHARING

1. Someone once said, "When we can't trace God we simply must trust Him." Turn to the person next to you and share a time when you've had difficulty trusting God.

2. St. Paul reminds us that "we know that in all things God works for the good of those who love Him." How do "we know" or on what basis do we place our trust in God?

3. We confess we love Him "because He first loved us" **(1 John 4:19).** In what special way did Jesus show His great love for us?

4. "In all things God works for the good…." Someone said this grand summary is "a soft pillow for a tired heart." In what way do these words serve as a soft pillow for your tired heart?

5. Is there someone you can think of who needs to have this "soft pillow" of assurance even now? How might you provide them with this pillow?

PRAYER

Lord God, when we can't trace You, help us to trust You. We do love You Lord. Forgive us for doubting at times that You are working Your good in all situations. Forgive us for the times we haven't trusted You (silently confess some of those times). As we meet together, come, bless us, assure us that "in all things" You will work for good. Through Jesus Christ our Lord. Amen.

Study 8

© 1994 CPH   Scripture references:NIV.

Neither Height Nor Depth

Romans 8:38–39

GOD'S WORD

For I am convinced that neither death nor life, neither angels nor demons, neither the present nor the future, nor any powers, neither height nor depth, nor anything else in all creation, will be able to separate us from the love of God that is in Christ Jesus our Lord. (Romans 8:38–39)

FOR SHARING

1. Have you ever felt separated from God and His love? When? Why?

2. St. Paul says in **Romans 8:37:** "No, in all these things we are more than conquerors through Him who loved us." With pen in hand underline all the powers that St. Paul says Christ has conquered.

3. "Neither height nor depth…will be able to separate us from the love of God." St. Paul is referring to the belief that astrological powers somehow influences events and behavior. What evidence do you see that many people, including Christians, sometimes have difficulty believing that heavenly bodies don't somehow influence their lives (e.g., superstition about Friday the 13th, reading the horoscope)? However, what does God's Word clearly proclaim about the influence of stars and other heavenly bodies? About "anything else in all creation"?

4. To be in Christ is to share His victory over all these powers. Read aloud another victory hymn of St. Paul's:

"Death has been swallowed up in victory. Where, O death, is your victory? Where, O death, is your sting?" The sting of death is sin, and the power of sin is the law. But thanks be to God! He gives us the victory through our Lord Jesus Christ.
(1 Cor. 15:54–57)

PRAYER

Heavenly Father, God of victories, we come to You,
to thank You for the victories You have given us over life and death; angels and demons; the present and the future; powers, height, and depth; and anything else in all creation;
to ask Your forgiveness for the times we have felt separated from You, for the times we have felt less than victorious over some of the worldly powers;
to ask Your help in all that we do so that we might be "more than conquerors through Him who loved us." In the name of Jesus. Amen.

Study 9

© 1994 CPH   Scripture references: NIV.

Love Is...
1 Corinthians 13:4

GOD'S WORD

Love is patient, love is kind. It does not envy, it does not boast, it is not proud. (1 Corinthians 13:4)

FOR SHARING

1. So-called experts have written books on the subject of love. Yet, all of what has been written is pale in comparison to the words of **1 Corinthians 13:4.** Why?

2. Liza Doolittle in "My Fair Lady" said, "Words, words, I'm tired of words. If you love me, show me!" According to St. Paul, what are some tangible ways to show your family love? the people at work? the people at church?

3. "Love is patient, love is kind" **(1 Corinthians 13:4a).** When do you find it most difficult to be kind: in moments of stress? when fatigued? in moments of failure? Why?

4. St. Paul reminds us, "Be kind and compassionate to one another, forgiving each other, just as in Christ God forgave you" **(Ephesians 4:32).** How does this verse speak to you in your relationship with family? friends? enemies?

5. A good way for a person to examine his or her love is to compare it to the words of **1 Corinthians 13:4.** If honest we must admit we deserve an "F." However, the good news is that God's love is kind. How kind? Read aloud **Ephesians 4:32** (found in the question above).

PRAYER

God of Love, when we think of love, we think of people You have placed in our lives who have exemplified the type of love St. Paul talked about. We remember especially...(silently name some of these people) and thank You for them. When we think about the love You have shown us, we recognize how pale our love for You and others is at times. Forgive us, Lord God. This week, make our love more patient, kinder, less envious, less boastful, and less proud. This we ask for Your love's sake. Amen.

Study 10

© 1994 CPH Scripture references:NIV.

Love As He Loves

1 Corinthians 13:7

GOD'S WORD

It [love] always protects, always trusts, always hopes, always perseveres. (1 Corinthians 13:7)

FOR SHARING

1. Love "always." St. Paul talks about "agape" love—unconditional love which comes from God. What do we know about God's love as evidenced in His sending Jesus to die for us?

2. In what ways is our love often different than God's?

3. M. Scott Peck writes in his best-selling book *The Road Less Traveled* (New York: Simon and Schuster, 1978, pp. 140-141):

"Children cannot grow to psychological maturity in an atmosphere of unpredictability, haunted by the specter of abandonment. Couples cannot resolve in any healthy way the universal issues of marriage—dependency and independence, dominance and submission, freedom and fidelity, for example—without the security of knowing that the act of struggling over these issues will not itself destroy the relationship."

(Copyright © 1978 by M. Scott Peck, M.D. Reprinted by permission of Simon & Shuster, Inc.)

What kinds of problems exist in relationships because people fail to love as God loves? How might demonstrating God's love overcome some of these problems?

4. As the Holy Spirit works through God's Word to strengthen our faith in Jesus, He empowers, motivates, and enables us to love as He loved us. What does this fact say about the importance of Bible study?

PRAYER

Lord God, lover of our souls,
we thank You for showing us a love that
  "always protects, always trusts, always hopes, always perseveres."
Forgive us for not demonstrating a love that
  "always protects, always trusts, always hopes, always perseveres."
Empower us with Your love to live a life demonstrating a love that
  "always protects, always trusts, always hopes, always perseveres."
Through Jesus Christ our Savior. Amen.

Study 11

© 1994 CPH   Scripture references:NIV.

A Lopsided Exchange

2 Corinthians 5:21

GOD'S WORD

God made Him who had no sin to be sin for us, so that in Him we might become the righteousness of God. (2 Corinthians 5:21)

FOR SHARING

1. Read aloud **2 Corinthians 5:21** several times. Then answer the following questions:

   a. What did God give us in exchange for our sins?

   b. How did He make such an exchange possible?

   c. Why would He make such a lopsided exchange?

2. Someone said, "He took my hell so that I might have His heaven!" Do you think it's even possible to truly comprehend such love? Try expressing His love in your own words.

3. What kind of response do you have to such a lopsided exchange and such extravagant love? Do you think your worship adequately reflects the praise and thanksgiving He deserves. Why? How might your worship better reflect the praise God deserves?

PRAYER

Silently meditate in prayer on the following two things: (1) God's lopsided exchange (our sin for His righteousness); (2) His tremendous love for us. Then give Him thanks. Pray the Lord's Prayer.

Study **12**

© 1994 CPH   Scripture references:NIV.

Transformed

Galatians 2:20

GOD'S WORD

I have been crucified with Christ and I no longer live, but Christ lives in me. The life I live in the body, I live by faith in the Son of God, who loved me and gave Himself for me. (Galatians 2:20)

FOR SHARING

1. St. Paul explains how Christ changed his life. He had lived by the Law by trying to win God's favor with the things He did, but found that he only felt greater separation from God. What is the purpose of the Law?

2. St. Paul says that he's different than what he once was. God changed him. How does Paul describe his transformation? Who now lived in St. Paul?

3. To the Christians of Rome, St. Paul writes: "Or don't you know that all of us who were baptized into Christ Jesus were baptized into His death? We were therefore buried with Him through baptism into death in order that, just as Christ was raised from the dead through the glory of the Father, we too may live a new life" **(Romans 6:3–4)**. St. Paul could not forget the day he received new life. Do you know the date of your baptism? Why is it an important date for you to remember? What happened then?

4. In what way does living "by faith in the Son of God, who loved (us) and gave himself for (us)" change the way you live? Regarding the keeping of the law? Regarding your worship? Regarding the way you treat those around you?

PRAYER

Jesus, I have been crucified with You and I no longer live, but You live in me. The life I live in the body, I live by faith in You O Jesus, who loved me and gave Himself for me. A thousand thanks and even more. Amen.

Study 13

© 1994 CPH   Scripture references: NIV.

His Wound=Our Joy

Isaiah 53:4–5

God's Word

Surely He took up our infirmities and carried out sorrows, yet we considered Him stricken by God, smitten by Him, and afflicted. But He was pierced for our transgressions, He was crushed for our iniquities; the punishment that brought us peace was upon Him, and by His wounds we are healed. (Isaiah 53:4–5)

For Sharing

1. Though the people of Israel had been disobedient, God gave words of comfort to them through the prophet Isaiah. He declared that God was going to send a Savior—one who would forgive them and give them eternal life. With pen in hand, underline how Jesus was going to bring about forgiveness and eternal life.

2. We often hear of people who wait for organ transplants. Why do some of these people die waiting? Would you ever consider giving one of your organs in order to save the life of another? Though many of us would not come forward to offer any of our organs for the sake of another, what did Jesus willingly do? What were the results?

3. Why was Jesus pierced? Why was He crushed? What did His punishment bring us? How were we healed?

4. A mother took her little boy along to the Sunday school teachers' meeting. On the way home the little boy said, "Mother, what kind of meeting were we at?" "Son, it was a Sunday school teachers' meeting." The little boy thought for a while and then asked, "Well, if it was a Sunday school teachers' meeting, why did every one look so angry?"
If we have been healed "by His wounds," why do we sometimes fail to reflect joy?

Prayer

Lord God, "Surely,"
  Yes, "surely,"
  "He took up our infirmities,"
  Yes, all "our infirmities,"
  "And carried our sorrows,"
  Yes, all "our sorrows,"
  "Yet we considered him stricken by God,"
  Yes, "stricken,"
  "Smitten by Him,"
  Yes, "smitten by Him"
  "And afflicted."
  Yes, "afflicted."
  "But He was pierced for our transgressions,"
  Yes, "for (all) our transgressions,"
  "He was crushed for our iniquities,"
  Yes, "crushed for (all) our iniquities,"
  "The punishment that brought us peace was upon Him,
  "And by His wounds we are healed."
  Hallelujah! Amen.

Study 14

© 1994 CPH   Scripture references:NIV.

Resuscitated by Christ

Ephesians 2:8–9

GOD'S WORD

For it is by grace you have been saved, through faith—and this not from yourselves, it is the gift of God—not by works, so that no one can boast. (Ephesians 2:8–9)

FOR SHARING

1. It is not uncommon to hear people say things like, "I found Jesus Christ!" or "I accepted Jesus Christ into my heart!" According to St. Paul, is salvation something we find or accept? Why or why not?

2. In an earlier verse St. Paul said, "As for you, you were dead in your transgressions and sins" **(Ephesians 2:1).** If one is dead in "transgressions and sins," why is it necessary for God to take the initiative to resuscitate?

3. What is grace? What makes it truly a gift? Why do pride and a spirit of individualism make it difficult for us to receive His grace?

4. When we receive a special gift, what's our typical response? In what ways do we respond to God's grace?

PRAYER

Speak or sing these stanzas of "Amazing Grace! How Sweet the Sound"

> Amazing Grace! How sweet the sound
> That saved a wretch like me!
> I once was lost but now am found,
> Was blind but now I see.
>
> Through many dangers, toil, and snares
> I have already come;
> His grace has brought me safe so far,
> His grace will see me home.

© 1994 CPH   Scripture references: NIV.

Christ's Attitude

Philippians 2:5–8

GOD'S WORD

Your attitude should be the same as that of Christ Jesus: Who, being in very nature God, did not consider equality with God something to be grasped, but made Himself nothing, taking the very nature of a servant, being made in human likeness. And being found in appearance as a man, He humbled Himself and became obedient to death—even death on a cross! (Philippians 2:5–8)

FOR SHARING

1. Describe the "attitude" which Christ Jesus had and which St. Paul says we ought to have? Identify some of Jesus' trademarks and trademarks which we, His followers, also have?

2. What evidence do you see in society that more and more people have forgotten the attitude of humility?

3. In becoming "obedient to death—even death on a cross," what did Jesus achieve for the world?

4. The Holy Spirit, working through God's Word, will change our attitude to be more like Christ's. How might this attitude affect relationships within your church? your work place? your family?

PRAYER

Speak or sing this stanza of "Just as I Am, Without One Plea."

> Just as I am, without one plea
> But that Thy blood was shed for me
> And that Thou bidd'st me come to Thee,
> O Lamb of God, I come, I come.

O God, we bring to You: repentance for our pride; gratitude for Your forgiveness; requests for You to make us more like You.

In the sure certainty that You hear our every prayer, through Jesus Christ. Amen.

Study 16

© 1994 CPH Scripture references:NIV.

Rejoice!

Philippians 4:6–7

GOD'S WORD

Do not be anxious about anything, but in everything, by prayer and petition, with thanksgiving, present your requests to God. And the peace of God, which transcends all understanding, will guard your hearts and minds in Christ Jesus. (Philippians 4:6–7)

FOR SHARING

1. St. Paul told the Philippians to "rejoice in the Lord," even though he was sitting in jail facing an uncertain future **(Philippians 4:4).** What events in your life threaten to rob you of your joy? If so, what does St. Paul suggest we do?

2. Do you remember a time as a child when you were scared or hurt? Do you remember a time when your father or mother sat down with you, embraced you, and told you everything would be all right? How did that make you feel? In what way does Your heavenly Father help you during difficult times?

3. We rejoice because Jesus Christ delivered us from our most serious troubles—sin, death, and the power of the devil. He died on the cross, giving up His very life, to pay for our sins. Since Jesus did that for us, what assurance do we have **(Romans 8:32)**?

4. What does God invite us to bring to Him in prayer?

5. What does He promise in **Philippians 4:7?** Why does His peace "transcend (human) understanding"?

PRAYER

Lord Jesus,
You have given us reason to rejoice. We thank You specifically for...
You have given us the assurance that we do not have to be "anxious about anything, but in everything, by prayer and petition, with thanksgiving, present (our) requests to (You)."
We do that now, specifically asking...
You have given us the assurance that "the peace of God, which transcends all understanding, will guard (our) hearts and minds in Christ Jesus." Grant this in the name of Jesus Christ. Amen.

Study 17

I Can with Christ

Philippians 4:13

GOD'S WORD

I can do everything through Him who gives me strength. (Philippians 4:13)

FOR SHARING

1. Why do people find it easier to say "I cannot" than "I can"? As sinful human beings, in what ways are "I can't" statements correct?

2. Jesus said, "I am the vine; you are the branches. If a man remains in Me and I in him, he will bear much fruit; apart from Me you can do nothing." **(John 15:5)**. "…Apart from [Jesus, we] can do nothing," but with Jesus Christ, what does St. Paul say we can do?

3. Just as God supplied a way of salvation through the death and resurrection of His only begotten Son, Jesus Christ, so He supplies us with what we need when we face difficulties in our lives. Share with another person a specific difficulty you're experiencing now? Have you asked God to give you strength to face this difficult situation?

PRAYER

Lord God, You assure us we "can do everything through [You] who gives [us] strength." However, we confess we do not always act like we believe Your promise. Too often, we say "cannot" instead of "we can." Forgive us. Even now we think of some special concerns we have. (Silently make these concerns known to the Lord asking that He give you strength to meet these challenges.) Through Jesus Christ. Amen.

Study 18

© 1994 CPH   Scripture references:NIV.

He's Coming Again

1 Thessalonians 4:13–18

GOD'S WORD

Brothers, we do not want you to be ignorant about those who fall asleep, or to grieve like the rest of men, who have no hope. We believe that Jesus died and rose again and so we believe that God will bring with Jesus those who have fallen asleep in Him. According to the Lord's own word, we tell you that we who are still alive, who are left till the coming of the Lord, will certainly not precede those who have fallen asleep. For the Lord Himself will come down from heaven, with a loud command, with the voice of the archangel and with the trumpet call of God, and the dead in Christ will rise first. After that, we who are still alive and are left will be caught up together with them in the clouds to meet the Lord in the air. And so we will be with the Lord forever. Therefore encourage each other with these words. (1 Thessalonians 4:13–18)

FOR SHARING

1. Is it wrong to grieve the loss of a loved one? Why do Christians not "grieve like the rest of men"?

2. On what does St. Paul base his teaching? On what must our teaching about God be based on?

3. Describe in your own words what you think the second coming of Christ will be like? Does the thought of His coming frighten you? If so, why? If not, why not? What words of comfort does St. Paul provide to us who have faith in Jesus?

PRAYER

Come Lord Jesus, grant us
> gratitude for the assurance that we do not "grieve like the rest of men, who have no hope" because of Jesus' death and resurrection **(1 Thessalonians 4:13b).**

Come Lord Jesus, grant us
> sorrow for our failure to look to Your precious Word for guidance and direction.

Come Lord Jesus, grant us
> trust in Your promises, that You will return and take us to be with You forever.

Through Jesus Christ our Lord. Amen.

Study 19

© 1994 CPH Scripture references:NIV.

With Confidence

Hebrews 4:16

GOD'S WORD

Let us then approach the throne of grace with confidence, so that we may receive mercy and find grace to help us in our time of need. (Hebrews 4:16)

FOR SHARING

1. Though Good Friday was not good for Jesus Christ, it was very good for us. On this day God redeemed us, purchased us back from sin and death. Jesus Christ, through His death, destroyed the barrier between God and people. What can we do now according to Hebrews 4:16? Why do Christians quite often include the phrase "in Jesus' name" as they conclude their prayers?

2. What does the writer tell us we receive as we approach His "throne of grace"? Why do we need mercy and grace?

3. Share with a partner special needs and concerns you have right now. Then ask him or her to pray for you this week, bringing before the Lord these special needs and concerns.

PRAYER

O God, our Father,
we come boldly with confidence grateful for Your gifts and sorry for our sins;
we come boldy with confidence to receive mercy and grace to help us in our need, especially...;
we come boldly in the name of Jesus Christ who through His death and resurrection makes all things possible. Amen.

Study 20

© 1994 CPH   Scripture references:NIV.

Faith Is...

Hebrews 11:1

GOD'S WORD

Now faith is being sure of what we hope for and certain of what we do not see. (Hebrews 11:1)

FOR SHARING

1. The writer clarifies that faith is more than a leap into the dark. In what way does he see faith more like a child running into the arms of a loving father?

2. Define your personal faith by completing the following phrase: "My faith is..." As you think of the many people of faith described in the Bible, which one would you say is most like you (e.g., David? Abraham? Enoch?).

3. The Old Testament saints such as Abraham and Noah were men of great faith because they believed God's promise of a Savior. We are a New Testament people who have seen the promise of a Savior fulfilled in the life, death, and resurrection of Jesus Christ. In the Greek language "hope" is more than wishful thinking. It is certainty based on God's assurances. In what way do God's promises present new possibilities for us? Through faith, what do we now have to look forward to?

PRAYER

O God, our Father, grant us faith
 that is "sure of what we hope for and certain of what we do not see";
 that believes in Your promises;
 that accepts Your Word as truth;
 that is loyal to You in good times and bad times.
In the name of Jesus, the risen Lord. Amen.

Study 21

© 1994 CPH   Scripture references: NIV.

More Than Words

James 2:14–17

GOD'S WORD

What good is it, my brothers, if a man claims to have faith but has no deeds? Can such faith save him? Suppose a brother or sister is without clothes and daily food. If one of you says to him, "Go, I wish you well; keep warm and well fed," but does nothing about his physical needs, what good is it? In the same way, faith by itself, if it is not accompanied by action, is dead. (James 2:14–17)

FOR SHARING

1. James wrote to Jewish converts who had been scattered as a result of persecution. Some of these Christians may have suggested that because of their faith in Jesus Christ they no longer had to be concerned about good works. What does James say to clarify any misunderstanding?

2. Share some illustrations that prove that love consists of more than words.

3. Paul said, "... Righteousness from God comes through faith in Jesus Christ to all who believe" **(Romans 3:22).** Faith, however, is not just intellectual. It is in a person's heart and affects all of his or her life. If you were arrested for being a Christian, would there be enough evidence to prove you guilty?

PRAYER

Lord God, we come to You because we want
    to give You thanks for coming to us with more than words of love but with
        actions of love—the very giving of Your Son Jesus Christ into death for our
        sins;
    to ask Your forgiveness for failing at times to back up our words of love with
        actions;
    to love You better so that actions of love might accompany our
        words of love.
We ask You to deepen our faith, our love, and strengthen our service as the Holy Spirit works through Your Word. For Jesus' sake. Amen.

Study 22

© 1994 CPH   Scripture references: NIV.

A Glimpse into Our Future

1 John 3:1–2

GOD'S WORD

How great is the love the Father has lavished on us, that we should be called children of God! And that is what we are! The reason the world does not know us is that it did not know Him. Dear friends, now we are children of God, and what we will be has not yet been made known. But we know that when He appears, we shall be like Him, for we shall see Him as He is. (1 John 3:1–2)

FOR SHARING

1. Speak aloud **1 John 3:1** in the way you think John would have spoken these words. Why do you think God's love amazed him so?

2. When and how did you become one of His children?

3. Being children of God has great meaning not only for our present but also for our future. God provides us a glimpse of our future with Him in His Word. Describe in your own words our future in Christ.

PRAYER

Lord God, "How great is the love [You have] lavished on us, that we should be called [Your] children!…And that is what we are!" Thanks be to You, O Lord. "We are [Your] children, and what we will be has not yet been made known. But we know that when [You] appear, we shall be like [You], for we shall see [You] as [You are]." We look forward to the day. Through Jesus Christ our Lord. Amen.

Study 23

© 1994 CPH   Scripture references:NIV.

What Will It Be Like?

Revelation 21:4

GOD'S WORD

He will wipe every tear from their eyes. There will be no more death or mourning or crying or pain, for the old order of things has passed away. (Revelation 21:4)

FOR SHARING

1. Man can live approximately 40 days without food, three days without water, eight minutes without air, but only a few seconds without hope. Why?

2. Through the tears of Jesus, His death, His mourning, His crying, His pain, we receive hope, assurance of forgiveness and eternal life. What does this hope consist of according to **Revelation 21:4?**

3. Which of the many things mentioned by John do you look forward to the most? What do you think it will be like to live without tears, without death, or mourning or crying or pain?

PRAYER

Speak or sing these stanzas of "I Know that My Redeemer Lives."

> I know that my Redeemer lives;
> What comfort this sweet sentence gives!
> He lives, He lives, who once was dead;
> He lives, my everliving Head.
>
> He lives to silence all my fears,
> He lives to wipe away my tears,
> He lives to calm my troubled heart,
> He lives all blessings to impart.
>
> He lives and grants me daily breath;
> He lives, and I shall conquer death;
> He lives my mansion to prepare;
> He lives to bring me safely there.

Bow your heads in prayer thanking God for your promised future.

Study **24**

© 1994 CPH   Scripture references: NIV.

It Turned Out Okay

Genesis 50:19–20

GOD'S WORD

"Don't be afraid....You intended to harm me, but God intended it for good to accomplish what is now being done, the saving of many lives." (Genesis 50:19–20)

FOR SHARING

1. Jacob favored his son Joseph. Because of this, his brothers' jealousy burned in hatred for him. In order to get rid of him, they sold him as a slave to a caravan of merchants who were on their way to Egypt. Though Egypt had a storehouse of evil awaiting Joseph, God was with him. After a great famine the brothers came to Joseph for food. They feared Joseph would kill them. But what did Joseph assure them?

2. In what way is the story of Joseph a shadow of an even greater story—the story of Jesus Christ? Though those jealous of Jesus sold Him and betrayed Him, how did God overrule all for the salvation of mankind?

3. Can you think of a time when the words of Joseph could have been your words? Can you recall another time in your life when things did not turn out as good as it did for Joseph? If so, reflect on the words of **1 Corinthians 13:12.** "Now we see but a poor reflection as in a mirror; then we shall see face to face. Now I know in part; then I shall know fully, even as I am fully known."

PRAYER

Lord God, we know the words of Joseph.
    With gratitude we thank You for working good in our lives.
    With confession we acknowledge that we sometimes doubt Your presence and Your working of good. Forgive us;
    with a request that you strengthen our faith so that we might be more confident of Your presence and Your working in our midst.
Through Jesus Christ, Lord and Savior, the one who was sold and betrayed, so that we might receive forgiveness for our many betrayals. Amen.

Study 25

© 1994 CPH   Scripture references: NIV.

Walking with God

Genesis 5:24

GOD'S WORD

Enoch walked with God; then he was no more, because God took him away. (Genesis 5:24)

FOR SHARING

1. The prophet Micah said that God demanded three things: (1) to act justly; (2) to love mercy; and (3) to walk humbly with God **(Micah 6:8).** How did Enoch's life reflect God's demands?

2. Describe in your own words what you think "walking with God" means? Name some ways in which people sometimes try to walk ahead of God? or behind Him? Enoch "walked with God." What were the results?

3. Enoch is listed in the book of Hebrews as one of God's faithful people. Because of his faith in a promised Savior—a Savior who would redeem mankind with His own death and resurrection—Enoch "pleased God" **(Hebrews 11:5–6).** By faith, is it possible for us to please God as well?

4. What happened to Enoch? Doesn't it seem logical that a man of such faith would be missed?

5. We also have faith in Jesus Christ. Remind yourself of what God will provide to you someday because of your faith in Jesus by adding your name to the passage: "_____ walked with God; then _____ was no more because God took _____ away."

PRAYER

Lord God, we come before You
    to thank You for the faith You have planted into our hearts;
    to plea for forgiveness for the times we have walked ahead or behind You;
    to ask that You help us to act justly, love mercy, and walk humbly with You.
Through Jesus Christ our Lord. Amen.

Study 26

© 1994 CPH Scripture references: NIV.

Falling Back in Love

Revelation 2:4–5

GOD'S WORD

"You have forsaken your first love. Remember the height from which you have fallen! Repent and do the things you did at first." (Revelation 2:4–5)

FOR SHARING

1. The story is told that when young Woolworth was ready for the grand opening of his first store he was in competition with another merchant down the street who had been in town for years. This merchant was not very happy with Woolworth opening a similar business, and so he placed the following advertisement in the paper: DO YOUR SHOPPING HERE! WE HAVE BEEN IN BUSINESS FOR OVER FIFTY YEARS! The next week, young Woolworth put his own advertisement into the local paper: DO YOUR SHOPPING HERE. WE'VE BEEN IN BUSINESS ONLY ONE WEEK. ALL OUR MERCHANDISE IS BRAND NEW*. His point was well made. Sometimes things do get old. What had gotten old in the church described in these verses from Revelation?

2. What three things does the writer recommend for "falling back in love"?

3. Meditate for a few seconds on your love relationship with God. Are you as in love with Him as you were five years ago or even a month ago? If not, why not?

4. Are there some sins that keep you from being totally committed to God? We need to remember "If we confess our sins, He is faithful and just and will forgive us our sins and purify us from all unrighteousness" **(1 John 1:9).** Jesus not only forgives us for not being in love, but also for not always behaving in love.

PRAYER

    Lord God, as we think back on our love for You,
        we remember…
        we repent of…
        we pledge to…
    through Jesus Christ our Lord. Amen.

* Excerpts taken from *Robert Schuller's Life Changes* edited by Robert A. Schuller. Copyright © 1981. Used by permission of Fleming H. Revell Company, a division of Baker Book House.

Will Life Ever Get Better?

Psalm 30:5

GOD'S WORD

For His anger lasts only a moment, but His favor lasts a lifetime; weeping may remain for a night, but rejoicing comes in the morning. (Psalm 30:5)

FOR SHARING

1. A troubled individual went to a psychiatrist for help with his depression. The psychiatrist listened attentively to the young man talk about his anxiety. After listening for a while the doctor advised the man to get out of the house and stop dwelling on his depression. He suggested that he go to the circus which had just arrived in town. "I understand," said the doctor, "there's a very funny clown in the show which has everyone rolling in the aisles with laughter. He'll surely help you!" The young man looked sadly at the doctor and said, "Doctor, I am the clown!"

Do you know people who often look happy and can make others laugh, but who are often inwardly sad and depressed? Have you ever heard anyone say, "I don't care if I live or die!" or "I wish I was dead!"? What circumstances might make dying seem better than life?

2. Some people may ask, "Will life ever be any better?" What assurance does the psalmist give us?

3. What does the psalmist remind us about God's anger? about his favor? about our weeping?

4. The events of Good Friday saddened the disciples. The one they had followed—Jesus Christ—had died. They probably asked, "Will life ever get better?" What joy did God provide three days later?

PRAYER

Spend some time talking to the Lord about the following things:
- thanks for the promise of **Psalm 30:5;**
- confession of your failing to trust in God's promise;
- guidance in lifting others up with the promise.

Study 28

© 1994 CPH   Scripture references:NIV.

Jesus' Great "Not!"

Psalm 23:1–6

GOD'S WORD

The Lord is my shepherd, I shall not be in want. He makes me lie down in green pastures, He leads me beside quiet waters, He restores my soul. He guides me in paths of righteousness for His name's sake. Even though I walk through the valley of the shadow of death, I will fear no evil, for You are with me; Your rod and Your staff, they comfort me. You prepare a table before me in the presence of my enemies. You anoint my head with oil; my cup overflows. Surely goodness and love will follow me all the days of my life, and I will dwell in the house of the Lord forever. (Psalm 23:1–6)

FOR SHARING

1. Reread this familiar psalm substituting your name for the pronouns "I" and "me" the author, David, used to describe his relationship to the Lord.

2. People today sometimes use the word "Not!" to indicate their disagreement or discomfort with a statement. Read the psalm again and with pen in hand, write "Not!" next to statements with which at times you may feel uncomfortable or disagree. Explain why.

3. God understands our "Not!" He sent His only Son Jesus to live, suffer, and die on the cross for all of the times we say and feel "Not!" to Him and His Word. Jesus said "Not!" to death when He rose from the grave. Jesus' great "Not!" enables us to confess the words David wrote in this psalm. Reread the psalm again. This time draw a heart around each of the "Nots!" you wrote.

4. How can remembering the empty tomb enable you to overcome the times when you are inclined to say "Not!" to God's Word and/or promises?

PRAYER

Confess the times when you have said "Not!" to God's Word.

Praise God for sending Jesus, who after dying on the cross said "Not!" to death by His resurrection. Praise Him for the assurance Jesus' "Not!" provides you when you feel burdened by sin or fear death.

Ask God to empower you to share Jesus' "Not!" to death with someone who has not confessed Jesus as his or her Lord and Savior.

Thank God for the assurance of His love and presence that enables you to confess the words of **Psalm 23**.

Study 29

© 1994 CPH   Scripture references:NIV.

Our Refuge and Strength

Psalm 46:1–2

GOD'S WORD

God is our refuge and strength, an ever-present help in trouble. Therefore we will not fear, though the earth give way and the mountains fall into the heart of the sea. (Psalm 46:1–2)

FOR SHARING

1. Read each of the following statements. Who or what has become the refuge for the person who made the statement?

"After three or four drinks, okay maybe five drinks, I forget about my stinking job."

"When Pat and I got married, everything was great. Now, after 10 years, things are just not the same. I'm ready for a change."

"I know I don't always have time to spend with my family. But the long hours of work enables me to give them everything they need."

"When I get down, I shop."

2. To whom or what do you often flee for refuge when you become overwhelmed, frustrated, angry, or disillusioned? Share a statement you have heard that indicates someone is fleeing for refuge to someone or something other than God.

3. Often we flee to people or things for refuge. These may give us temporary relief, but can never provide us with the long-lasting relief God offers. In fact, seeking refuge and strength from things or people leads us away from God. What permanent relief does God offer to us even when we seek refuge and strength from other people or things?

4. God's love and forgiveness for us in Christ is "our refuge and strength, an ever-present help in trouble." Keep in mind Jesus' love for you as you complete the following sentence from the psalm:

Therefore we [I] will not fear, though…(include situations from your life that overwhelm you, frustrate you, make you angry, or disillusion you)…, because God loves me so much that He even sent His Son Jesus to suffer and die on the cross for me.

PRAYER

Confess the things to which you flee for refuge and strength.

Thank God for His forgiveness through Jesus for relying on people and things to provide you refuge.

Praise God for enabling you to flee to Him for refuge and strength in all situations—good and bad—in our lives.

Ask God to help you demonstrate His compassion to people who rely upon things or people for refuge.

Study **30**

© 1994 CPH Scripture references: NIV.

A Lamp and a Light

Psalm 119:105

GOD'S WORD

Your word is a lamp to my feet and a light for my path. (Psalm 119:105)

FOR SHARING

1. Paul searched for a flashlight after the power went out.
Have you ever tried to find something in the dark? If so, what? Why is searching for something in the dark often frustrating?

2. After 45 minutes of groping through drawers, Paul found the flashlight. He pushed the button eager to have light once again. The batteries were dead.
Describe Paul's feelings.

3. How important is light? What might life be like without lamps?

4. The psalmist compares God's Word to a lamp to his feet and a light to his path. In His Word God tells us what to do and what not to do in order to live our lives to the fullest. Just as a light and lamp guide us in darkness, so God's Word guides us in a world darkened by sin.
God also reveals His plan of salvation for us in His Word. Because of sin we do the things He tells us not to do and don't do the things He tells us to do. However, God's Word assures us of our rescue from the darkness of sin through His Son Jesus, the Light of the World.
How does Jesus provide light to your life, so often darkened by sin? How does the Light of the world affect what you do and say?

PRAYER

Give thanks to God for the Light He provided to a world darkened by sin.
Ask God to give you a zeal to study His Word, so that through faith strengthened by the Holy Spirit you might do that which He tells you to do and not do those things He tells you not to do.
Praise God for opportunities you have to share His Light with others who continue to live in darkness.

© 1994 CPH   Scripture references:NIV.

What's Your Grade?

Proverbs 3:5–6

God's Word

Trust in the Lord with all your heart and lean not on your own understanding; in all your ways acknowledge Him, and He will make your paths straight. (Proverbs 3:5–6)

For Sharing

1. Solomon, the author of these two short verses, commands us to do three things. Underline each command. Then evaluate your ability to accomplish each of Solomon's commands with A–superior; B–very good; C–average; D–below average; or F–failing.

2. God expects us to always get an A. Jesus shared God's expectation in His sermon on the mount, when He said, "Be perfect" **(Matthew 5:48).** Evaluate your ability to accomplish God's expectation with an A, B, C, D, or F.

3. God knew that on our own we would be unable to get an A. That's why He sent Jesus. Jesus lived a perfect life. He received an A. Jesus went willingly to the cross to suffer and die for our F. Jesus took an F, so we could receive an A. Jesus' love motivates and strengthens us so that we can trust Him, lean not on our own understanding, and acknowledge Him in all our ways. For Jesus' sake God makes our paths straight, even when we choose to take a crooked path.

What are some ways we can respond to God's love for us in Christ in our relationships within our families? with people within in our congregation? with people who do not know Jesus as their Lord and Savior?

Prayer

Review each of the commands in the proverb. Before each command write, "Jesus, enable me with Your love to…" Change the word "your" to "my." Now, pray the proverb with those changes assured that because of Jesus, God will provide you with an A.

Study 32

© 1994 CPH   Scripture references: NIV.

Jesus Swallowed Death

Isaiah 25:8–9

GOD'S WORD

He will swallow up death forever. The Sovereign Lord will wipe away the tears from all faces; He will remove the disgrace of His people from all the earth. The Lord has spoken. In that day they will say, "Surely this is our God; we trusted in Him, and He saved us. This is the Lord, we trusted in Him; let us rejoice and be glad in His salvation." (Isaiah 25:8–9)

FOR SHARING

1. The little boy who had been swinging on the swing suddenly began to choke. The mother ran to her son's aid and asked, "What's wrong?" The boy, now gagging, replied, "I swallowed a fly."
   Have you ever swallowed something unpleasant? If so, what?

2. The Bible verses indicate that He, Jesus, swallowed something unpleasant for us. What did Jesus swallow? When and how did Jesus swallow this?

3. Because Jesus swallowed up death forever, what unpleasant thing will we never have to taste? How does God "wipe away the tears" from our faces?

4. According to Isaiah, what can we say today, tomorrow, and everyday in the future, including the day when we pass from this life into eternity with Jesus?

PRAYER

Thank God for sending Jesus to swallow up death forever.
Praise God for wiping away the tears from our faces by assuring us that death will not swallow us.
Ask God to provide you with new opportunities to share with unbelievers the confidence He provides, even as you anticipate death, through Jesus Christ.

Study 33

© 1994 CPH Scripture references: NIV.

Do You Not Know?!?

Isaiah 40:28–31

GOD'S WORD

Do you not know? Have you not heard? The Lord is the everlasting God, the Creator of the ends of the earth. He will not grow tired or weary, and His understanding no one can fathom. He gives strength to the weary and increases the power of the weak. Even youths grow tired and weary, and young men stumble and fall; but those who hope in the Lord will renew their strength. They will soar on wings like eagles; they will run and not grow weary, they will walk and not be faint. (Isaiah 40:28–31)

FOR SHARING

1. Read emphatically the two questions Isaiah asks at the beginning of these verses. Write an exclamation mark after each question to indicate the surprise Isaiah must have had as He asked God's people these questions.

2. Underline twice each of the statements about the Lord—His attributes and His actions on behalf of His people.

3. Think about a time in your life when Isaiah could have confronted you with these same questions (e.g., a time when you felt afraid, abandoned, lonely, helpless, weary, unable to cope, distant from God, etc.).

4. Satan, the world, and our own sinful nature would have us believe that God doesn't care or won't help. At those times God confronts us with His Word, "Do you not know? Have you not heard?" Then God assures us in His Word of His forgiveness through Jesus for doubting Him and His presence. His love for us strengthens us to "soar on wings of eagles…run and not grow weary…walk and not be faint."

PRAYER

Confess your failure to trust in God above all things.
Give thanks to God for the forgiveness He provides for all sins through faith in Jesus.
Ask God to strengthen you as the Holy Spirit works through God's Word to confront your sin and to assure you of Jesus' forgiveness.
Ask God to provide you with an opportunity to share these verses from Isaiah with someone who feels weak, tired, or weary.
Thank God for giving strength to the weary and power to the weak.

Study 34

© 1994 CPH   Scripture references:NIV.

Drowning in...

Isaiah 41:10

GOD'S WORD

So do not fear, for I am with you; do not be dismayed, for I am your God. I will strengthen you and help you; I will uphold you with My righteous right hand. (Isaiah 41:10)

FOR SHARING

1. People who don't know how to swim need a life preserver. Without a life preserver, a nonswimmer would drown in deep water.

Often in this life we may feel that we are drowning; drowning in our troubles, drowning in uncertainties, drowning in fear, drowning in our sin and its consequences. Share a time when you felt that you were treading water and about to go under.

2. What does God offer in **Isaiah 41:10** to those who feel they are about to drown? The "right hand of God" refers to God's awesome power. How does knowing that God holds out His right hand to you comfort you when troubles threaten to drown you?

3. To what things might we cling, other than God, as we face troubles, hardships, and/or difficult decisions?

4. God continues to offer us His outstretched hand, even when we grasp hold of things other than Him. For Jesus' sake He forgives our attempts to go it alone. His love for us enables us to grasp His right hand and hold tight to it as we experience difficulties in this life. What comfort does Jesus holding on to us with His right hand give us as we face situations that might cause us to feel we are drowning?

PRAYER

Confess our sinful desire to go it alone.

Thank God for His forgiveness in Jesus and His ever-present desire for us to grasp hold of His hand and walk with Him.

Praise God for strengthening us and upholding us in good, as well as bad times.

Ask God to enable you to reach out to those people who need to experience the power of God's righteous right hand in their lives.

Study 35

© 1994 CPH   Scripture references: NIV.

Purchased Back

Isaiah 43:1

God's Word

But now, this is what the Lord says—He who created you, O Jacob, He who formed you, O Israel: "Fear not, for I have redeemed you; I have summoned you by name; you are Mine." (Isaiah 43:1)

For Sharing

1. What ownership does God claim in this verse from Isaiah?

2. Substitute your name for "you" in the quote. You belong to God. God owns you. What did God do for you in order to claim ownership?

3. The word "redeem" means "to purchase back." The God who created you loves you so much that He purchased you back from sin and death. What price did God have to pay to redeem you? *Hint:* St. Paul writes, "He [God]…did not spare His own Son, but gave Him up for us all" **(Romans 8:32).**

4. Since God claims ownership of you, you can claim ownership of the blessings His Son earned for you on the cross. List those blessings.

5. What might you say to someone who has rejected God's ownership? Begin your response by sharing what God's ownership provides to you.

Prayer

> Forgive me Lord for…
> Thank You Lord for…
> Lord, give me…
> I praise You Lord for…
> In Jesus' name I pray. Amen.

Study 36

© 1994 CPH Scripture references:NIV.

Talking to a Wall

Isaiah 55:10–11

GOD'S WORD

As the rain and the snow come down from heaven, and do not return to it without watering the earth and making it bud and flourish, so that it yields seed for the sower and bread for the eater, so is My word that goes out from My mouth: It will not return to Me empty, but will accomplish what I desire and achieve the purpose for which I sent it. (Isaiah 55:10–11)

FOR SHARING

1. Share a time when after talking with someone you thought, "I might as well have been talking to a wall."

2. When Christians share their faith in Jesus with unbelievers, they might conclude by the person's response or lack of response that they have failed, "talked to a wall." What responses from an unbeliever might cause a Christian to conclude this?

3. The devil likes nothing more than to convince us that our witness of faith to an unbeliever is inadequate. What can Satan accomplish if he can make us believe our ability to tell others about Jesus is a failure?

4. God's promise to us in these two verses from Isaiah are just as sure as His promise, "If we confess our sins, He is faithful and just and will forgive us our sins and purify us from all unrighteousness" **(1 John 1:9).** What promise does God make to those of us who share God's love with unbelievers? How does this provide us hope and comfort?

PRAYER

Pray that the Holy Spirit would continually remind you of God's promises, including the promise that God's Word "will not return to Me empty." Pray that God would use you to share boldly your faith in Jesus. Confess your failures to witness because of fear of rejection or concern over your ability. Thank God for His continual love for you and forgiveness for your sins in Jesus.

Study 37

© 1994 CPH   Scripture references: NIV.

Good News

Isaiah 61:1–3

GOD'S WORD

The Spirit of the Sovereign Lord is on me, because the Lord has anointed me to preach good news to the poor. He has sent me to bind up the brokenhearted, to proclaim freedom for the captives and release from darkness for the prisoners, to proclaim the year of the Lord's favor and the day of vengeance of our God, to comfort all who mourn, and provide for those who grieve in Zion—to bestow on them a crown of beauty instead of ashes, the oil of gladness instead of mourning, and a garment of praise instead of a spirit of despair. They will be called oaks of righteousness, a planting of the Lord for the display of His splendor. (Isaiah 61:1–3)

FOR SHARING

1. Share some good news you have heard recently.

2. How do you respond to good news?

3. Isaiah does what many people do when they hear good news—he tells others. What good news does he share?

4. Compare the good news Isaiah shares to the news shared in the following New Testament passages.
"You have been set free from sin and have become slaves to righteousness" **(Romans 6:18).**

"But you are a chosen people, a royal priesthood, a holy nation, a people belonging to God, that you may declare the praises of Him who called you out of darkness into His wonderful light" **(1 Peter 2:9).**

"He will wipe every tear from their eyes. There will be no more death or mourning or crying or pain, for the old order of things has passed away" **(Revelation 21:4).**

Through faith in Christ Jesus God has proclaimed freedom to us from the bondage of sin, overcome the darkness of our sin through the Light of the world, and comforted all who mourn with the gift of eternal life.

PRAYER

Thank God for the Good News of a Savior.
Thank God for the people who share the Good News of a Savior with us.
Ask for God's power to enable us to tell others His Good News.

Study 38

© 1994 CPH   Scripture references: NIV.

Forgive and Forget

Jeremiah 31:34

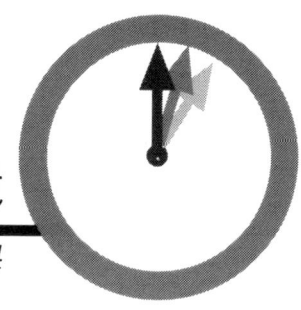

GOD'S WORD

"No longer will a man teach his neighbor, or a man his brother, saying, 'Know the Lord,' because they will all know Me, from the least of them to the greatest," declares the Lord. "For I will forgive their wickedness and will remember their sins no more." (Jeremiah 31:34)

FOR SHARING

1. "I can forgive, but I can't forget." What hidden meaning might you find in this often used statement? Is it possible to forgive and forget? Or will you always remember that which you forgive? What might be the danger of forgiving and forgetting? of forgiving, but not forgetting? of forgetting, but not forgiving?

2. What might we fear if God said, "I forgive you, but I won't forget your sin?" How would this affect you as you think about Judgment Day?

3. What does Jeremiah say the Lord promises to do? What comfort do we receive from knowing that God in Christ not only forgives us, but also forgets our wickedness?

PRAYER

Pray that God would enable all people to know Him and His love for all people.
Praise God for the assurance that He not only forgives our sins but also forgets them.
Ask God to help us not only forgive those who hurt us but also forget what they did or didn't do.

Study 39

© 1994 CPH   Scripture references: NIV.

Feet Like a Deer

Habbakuk 3:19

GOD'S WORD

The Sovereign Lord is my strength; He makes my feet like the feet of a deer, He enables me to go on the heights. (Habbakuk 3:19)

FOR SHARING

1. When, if ever, would you like to have feet like a deer?

2. Consider the following:
A deer is sure-footed. It can maneuver steep, narrow, and/or rocky places with confidence.
A deer is swift-footed. It can flee from danger without fear that a predator can and will catch it.
Complete the following sentence:
Since God promises to make my feet like a deer, I can

3. What comfort can I get from Habakkuk's words when sin, Satan, or the world threaten to overcome me?

4. Compare Habakkuk's words to St. Paul's words, "For I am convinced that neither death nor life, neither angels nor demons, neither the present nor the future, nor any powers, neither height nor depth, nor anything else in all creation, will be able to separate us from the love of God that is in Christ Jesus our Lord" **(Romans 8:38–39).**

PRAYER

Complete the following for a closing prayer.
The Sovereign Lord is my strength; He makes my feet…like the feet of a deer. Therefore, I…

Study 40

© 1994 CPH   Scripture references:NIV.

What's First?

Matthew 6:33

GOD'S WORD

But seek first His kingdom and His righteousness, and all these things will be given to you as well. (Matthew 6:33)

FOR SHARING

1. What comes first in your life? Rank the following items with 1 being most important.
   - ____ job
   - ____ family
   - ____ self
   - ____ money
   - ____ God
   - ____ happiness
   - ____ other

2. The First Commandment states, "You shall have no other gods." People have other gods when they regard and worship any creature or thing as God; when they believe in a god who is not the triune God; *when they fear, love, or trust in any person or thing as they should fear, love, and trust in God alone;* and when they join in the worship of one who is not the triune God.

   How do we disobey God when anything or anyone other than God comes first in our life?

3. What does Jesus promise to those who fear, love, and trust in God above all things?

4. God knew that because of our sinful nature we would seek first things other than Him. St. Paul summarizes the struggle between doing what God desires and what our sinful nature desires.

   "I do not understand what I do. For what I want to do I do not do, but what I hate I do…I know that nothing good lives in me, that is, in my sinful nature. For I have the desire to do what is good, but I cannot carry it out. For what I do is not the good I want to do; no, the evil I do not want to do—this I keep on doing…Who will rescue me from this body of death? Thanks be to God—through Jesus Christ our Lord!" (selected verses from **Romans 7:15–25).**

   Who rescues us from the desires of our sinful nature and enables us to "seek first His kingdom and His righteousness?"

PRAYER

Confess the words of St. Paul from **Romans 7.**

Ask the Holy Spirit to strengthen you as you study God's Word so that you might "seek first His kingdom and His righteousness."

Study 41

© 1994 CPH   Scripture references:NIV.

Forgetting the Obvious

Matthew 7:7

God's Word

"Ask and it will be given to you; seek and you will find; knock and the door will be opened to you." (Matthew 7:7)

For Sharing

1. People stand around looking at hallograms for hours, searching for that which is so obvious to others.

   Has anyone ever asked or told you something that was obvious? If so, what? The difficulty with judging the obvious is that what is obvious to me, may not be obvious at all to someone else.

2. Someone once said that Jesus' words in His Sermon on the Mount "beg the obvious." Do you agree or disagree? Why?

   Write Jesus' three illustrative statements in your own words.

3. As obvious as Jesus' statement might seem, how often do we forget or fail to ask, seek, and knock?

4. Do you agree or disagree with the following statement: "Our asking, seeking, and knocking is directly proportionate to the strength of our faith?" Why or why not?

5. Through the means of grace, God's Word and His Sacrament, the Holy Spirit works to strengthen our faith. As God strengthens our faith in Jesus, He enables us to ask, to seek, and to knock with greater frequency.

Prayer

Take time now as God's people whose faith has been strengthened through God's Word to
- Ask...Dear Lord, please...
- Seek...Dear Jesus, I seek to...
- Knock...Holy Spirit, open new doors so I might...

Study 42

© 1994 CPH   Scripture references: NIV.

Built on the Rock

Matthew 7:24–25

GOD'S WORD

"Therefore everyone who hears these words of Mine and puts them into practice is like a wise man who built his house on the rock. The rain came down, the streams rose, and the winds blew and beat against the house; yet it did not fall, because it had its foundation on the rock." (Matthew 7:24–25)

FOR SHARING

1. In these verses Jesus compares His Word to a house built on a rock. A person who listens to and believes in God's Word has a solid foundation of faith that cannot be shaken. What storms might challenge a Christian's faith?

2. Many churches have disregarded or challenged God's Word on various issues—abortion, euthanasia, homosexuality, etc. How does this disregard weaken the foundation of faith? How might questioning one portion of God's Word threaten all portions of it, including the central teaching of the Christian church—we have been saved by God's grace alone, through faith alone, in Christ alone?

3. St. Paul says, "All Scripture is God-breathed and is useful for teaching, rebuking, correcting and training in righteousness, so that the man of God may be thoroughly equipped for every good work" **(2 Timothy 3:16–17)**.
How might you use this Bible passage to respond to someone who said,
"The Word of God is useful, but not the ultimate authority."

"God's Word was written for people many years ago. We need to take those things that are relevant for today and discard those things that are no longer useful."

"God gave us minds. We should use them to determine what is truthful in Scripture and what is not."

PRAYER

Thank God for the solid foundation He has provided you in His Word.
Ask God to strengthen your faith so that you might defend His Word and its truth.
Praise God for revealing His love for you in Jesus Christ through His Word.

Study 43

In a Nutshell

John 3:16

GOD'S WORD

"For God so loved the world that He gave His one and only Son, that whoever believes in Him shall not perish but have eternal life." (John 3:16)

FOR SHARING

1. Even if they know no other Scripture passages, most people know **John 3:16.** Although we may be inclined to consider this passage overused, it contains a clear exposition of the Gospel.

   Restate the passage in your own words. This may be difficult to do, since the words are so familiar.

2. Why is it appropriate, even if a person knows no other Scripture passages, to know this one?

3. Why do you think **John 3:16** is often referred to as "the Gospel in a nutshell?" Does this phrase describe correctly the message of the Bible passage? Why or why not?

4. What would you say to someone who asks you to explain the message from God found in this passage?

PRAYER

   Thank You, God, for loving the world.
   Thank You, God, for giving Your one and only Son.
   Thank You, God, for giving me faith to believe.
   Thank You, God, for giving me the gift of eternal life.
   Enable me, Lord, to share this message with someone who does not know it or believe it.
   Help me, Lord, to never take its simple message for granted.

Study 44

© 1994 CPH Scripture references:NIV.

If Death Would Only Die...

John 11:25

GOD'S WORD

Jesus said to her, "I am the resurrection and the life. He who believes in Me will live, even though he dies." (John 11:25)

FOR SHARING

1. Someone once said as he reflected upon the death of a loved one, "If death would only die, then I could live again." React to this statement. Do you agree or disagree?

2. Why do you think this is a favorite Bible passage for a funeral sermon?

3. How do these words of Jesus affect you as you anticipate death someday?

4. How are Jesus' words from this Bible passage and Jesus' action on our behalf—His life, death, and resurrection—reflected in the following words of St. Paul?
   "Death has been swallowed up in victory."
   "Where, O death, is your victory?
   Where, O death, is your sting?" **(1 Corinthians 15:54–55).**

PRAYER

Sing or speak together these stanzas of "I Know that My Redeemer Lives."

I know that my Redeemer lives!
What comfort this sweet sentence gives!
He lives, He lives, who once was dead;
He lives, my everliving head!

He lives triumphant from the grave;
He lives eternally to save;
He lives exalted, throned above;
He lives to rule His church in love.

Study 45

© 1994 CPH   Scripture references: NIV.

Vine, Branches, and Fruit

John 15:5–7

GOD'S WORD

"I am the vine; you are the branches. If a man remains in Me and I in him, he will bear much fruit; apart from Me you can do nothing. If anyone does not remain in Me, he is like a branch that is thrown away and withers; such branches are picked up, thrown into the fire and burned. If you remain in Me and My words remain in you, ask whatever you wish, and it will be given you." (John 15:5–7)

FOR SHARING

1. Recently, my wife and I sent one dozen long-stemmed roses to my mother-in-law for her birthday. Three days after her birthday, my mother-in-law told us the roses were dead. We called the florist to complain about the short life of the roses. The florist said, "Roses don't live long after they are cut from the stem."
Compare the story of the roses with Jesus' story of the vine, branches, and fruit.

2. What occurs when we as branches fail to remain in the vine, Jesus? What evidence do you see in society that indicates people have failed to remain attached to the vine? What is the ultimate consequence for a branch that becomes detached from the vine?

3. What is Jesus' promise to those who remain in Him and His words?

4. We stay connected to Jesus, the vine, through God's Word. What does this say to us as Christians concerning the importance of regular Bible study, daily devotions, and attendance in worship?

5. Through faith strengthened by God's love for us in Jesus, as revealed in God's Word, the Holy Spirit empowers us to bear fruit. "But the fruit of the Spirit is love, joy, peace, patience, kindness, goodness, faithfulness, gentleness and self-control" **(Galatians 5:22–23).** What opportunities have you had recently to demonstrate the fruit of the Spirit?

PRAYER

Thank God for His grace that enabled you to become attached to the vine.
Praise God for His great love for you demonstrated by Jesus' death and resurrection.
Ask the Holy Spirit to provide you with new opportunities to bear the fruit of faith.

Study 46

© 1994 CPH Scripture references:NIV.

Two Big Words

Romans 3:23–24

GOD'S WORD

"For all have sinned and fall short of the glory of God, and are justified freely by His grace through the redemption that came by Christ Jesus." (Romans 3:23–24)

FOR SHARING

1. In these two short verses we find two very big words—justified and redemption—and one small word with a big meaning—grace. In order to understand the importance of what Paul says in these verses, we must first understand the meaning of these words.

    Justified means "made right." Jesus' death on the cross made us right before God. Since Jesus made us right, we must assume that before Jesus something was wrong between God and us. What was wrong?

    Redemption means "purchased or bought back." God bought us back from the slavery of sin through Jesus. What price did Jesus pay to purchase us back from sin?

    Grace is God's undeserved love for us. What did we deserve because of our sin? However, what does God provide to us by His grace through faith in Jesus?

2. In these verses St. Paul summarizes the heart and core of the Christian faith. Use your own words to summarize Paul's important message to the Christians in Rome.

PRAYER

We confess our sin before God.

We offer praise for the forgiveness He provides to us by His grace through faith in Jesus.

We give thanks that Jesus made us right before God and purchased us back from the slavery of sin.

We ask that You would enable us to proclaim boldly Your love for all people.

We give You praise and thanks for Your Son, our Savior, Jesus.

Study 47

© 1994 CPH Scripture references:NIV.

United We Stand, Divided We Fall

Romans 6:3–5

God's Word

"Or don't you know that all of us who were baptized into Christ Jesus were baptized into His death? We were therefore buried with Him through baptism into death in order that, just as Christ was raised from the dead through the glory of the Father, we too may live a new life. If we have been united with Him like this in His death, we will certainly also be united with Him in His resurrection." (Romans 6:3–5)

For Sharing

1. "United we stand, divided we fall." Can you demonstrate the truth of this statement in your relationships with family? with friends? within the congregation?

2. God united us with Jesus through Holy Baptism. What do we share with Jesus through this union?

3. Unfortunately, we often divide ourselves from Jesus. A popular bumper sticker says, "If you feel far away from God, guess who moved?" How can we divide or separate ourselves from God?

4. God invites us back to Him. He grants us forgiveness for the times we separate ourselves from Him. Through God's Word the Holy Spirit works to strengthen our unity with Christ through faith. How can we demonstrate our unity with Christ in our relationship with others?

Prayer

Lord God, may the unity You share with us through Christ Jesus,
    strengthen relationships within our family,
    strengthen relationships within our congregation,
    strengthen relationships among our friends,
so that in all our relationships we might have greater opportunity to share Your love for us in Christ. Amen.

Study 48

© 1994 CPH Scripture references: NIV.

Wages and Gifts

Romans 6:23

God's Word

For the wages of sin is death, but the gift of God is eternal life in Christ Jesus our Lord. (Romans 6:23)

For Sharing

1. What is the difference between earning a wage and receiving a gift?

2. What has our sin *earned* us?

3. What gift do we *receive* through Christ Jesus our Lord?

4. How would you respond to someone who said,
"Go to heaven? Well, I guess I'll go to heaven. I mean, I've tried to be a good person."

"I'm sure God loves me. At least I'm better than my next door neighbor who goes to church every Sunday."

"I deserve eternal life. I mean I've never been in major trouble."

Prayer

I confess that I deserve…
Thank You for giving me…
Enable me to tell others of the undeserved love You share freely with me.

Study 49

© 1994 CPH   Scripture references: NIV.

Do Good to All

Galatians 6:10

GOD'S WORD

Therefore, as we have opportunity, let us do good to all people, especially to those who belong to the family of believers. (Galatians 6:10)

FOR SHARING

1. In his letter to the churches in Galatia, Paul describes freedom in Christ as service to one another. Paul summarizes God's Law in the words, "Love your neighbor as yourself" **(Galatians 5:14)**. Keeping these truths in mind, explain Paul's statement, "as we have opportunity." When does a Christian have opportunity to serve others or love his or her neighbor?

2. Jesus defines neighbor as anyone with whom you might come into contact. What kind of a witness do we provide to unbelievers when we fail to love our neighbor outside the church? within the church?

3. As the Holy Spirit works through God's Word to strengthen our faith in Jesus, we produce fruit. St. Paul lists those fruit in **Galatians 5:22–23:** "But the fruit of the Spirit is love, joy, peace, patience, kindness, goodness, faithfulness, gentleness and self-control." How would demonstrating these fruit positively affect relationships within your family? with your friends? within your congregation?

4. Explore some new opportunities or possibilities to "do good to all people."

PRAYER

Ask God to provide you with new opportunities to "do good to all people."
Thank God for calling you into the family of believers.
Confess your sin that keeps you from loving your neighbor as yourself.
Praise God for the forgiveness He offers to all who believe in Jesus and the power to enable you to "love your neighbor as yourself."

Study 50

© 1994 CPH   Scripture references: NIV.

A Greater Inheritance

1 Peter 1:3–5

GOD'S WORD

"Praise be to the God and Father of our Lord Jesus Christ! In His great mercy He has given us new birth into a living hope through the resurrection of Jesus Christ from the dead, and into an inheritance that can never perish, spoil or fade—kept in heaven for you, who through faith are shielded by God's power until the coming of the salvation that is ready to be revealed in the last time." (1 Peter 1:3–5)

FOR SHARING

1. An attorney calls to inform you that a distant relative who died suddenly has included you in his will. The attorney invites you to be present at the reading of the will in three weeks. What might be your first reaction to the news? How might your feelings change as the day of the reading of the will draws closer? What might you do if you learn at the reading of the will that your distant relative has made you a millionaire?

2. What makes the inheritance that Jesus has earned for us unique? The inheritance that we claim through Jesus is greater than a million, or a billion, or even a trillion dollars. What is the difference between the inheritance we claim through Jesus and an earthly inheritance?

3. Peter responds to the inheritance by exclaiming, "Praise be to the God and Father of our Lord Jesus Christ!" What ways do you respond to the great inheritance given to you—the inheritance of forgiveness of sin and eternal life?

PRAYER

The last will and testament has been read. Let us
> praise God for providing us the inheritance that can never perish, spoil, or fade—eternal life through faith in Jesus;
> confess our failure to share with others our joy in the inheritance we claim through Jesus;
> thank God for sending Jesus to forgive us for all of our failures; and
> ask that the Holy Spirit would enable us to share with others the joy we claim in the inheritance Jesus won for us.

Study 51

God's Insurance Policy

Revelation 2:10

GOD'S WORD

Do not be afraid of what you are about to suffer. I tell you, the devil will put some of you in prison to test you, and you will suffer persecution for ten days. Be faithful, even to the point of death, and I will give you the crown of life. (Revelation 2:10)

FOR SHARING

1. The Holy Spirit inspired John to write Revelation to provide comfort and hope to Christians who faced cruel persecution by the Roman government for their faith in Jesus. Although most Christians are no longer persecuted by the government for their faith, they face a persecution more deadly and more cruel—persecution by Satan. What evidence do you see in your life, your community, and the world that Satan is waging a war against Christians?

2. While persecution by people can rob us of our physical life, persecution by Satan threatens our spiritual life. John reminds Christians to "be faithful." The Holy Spirit strengthens our faith through God's Word. Why is it so important that Christians study God's Word privately and publicly? How is remaining close to God through His Word like an insurance policy against Satan's persecution?

3. What does this passage promise to those who remain steadfast in their faith?

PRAYER

Sing or speak together these stanzas of "Crown Him with Many Crowns."

Crown Him with many crowns,
The Lamb upon His throne;
Hark how the heavenly anthem drowns
All music but its own.
Awake, my soul and sing
Of Him who died for thee,
And hail Him as thy matchless king
Through all eternity.

Crown Him the Lord of life,
Who triumphed o'er the grave
And rose victorious in the strife
For those He came to save.
His glories now we sing,
Who died and rose on high,
Who died eternal life to bring
And lives that death may die.

Study 52

For more in-depth adult Bible studies...

Find Healing in...

Christian Support Studies for Individuals or Groups

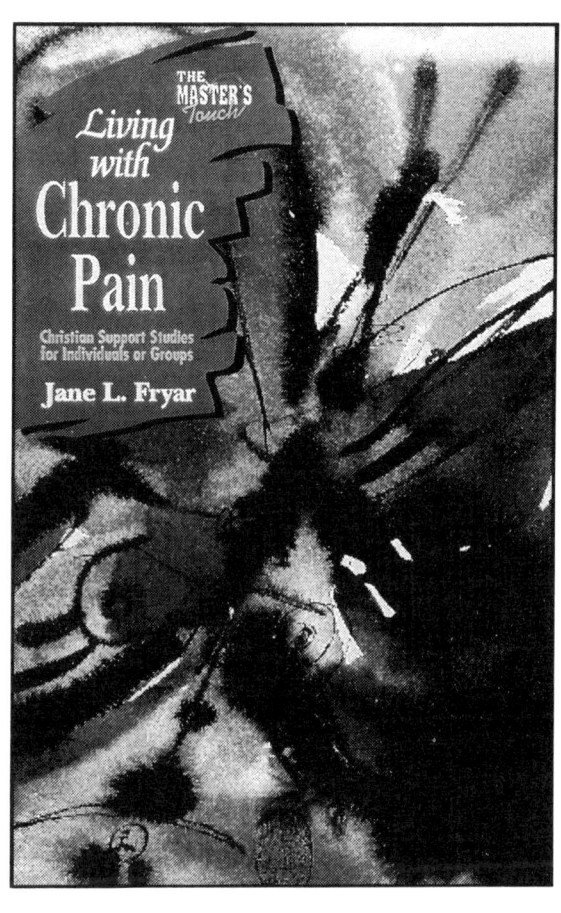

Jesus' healing touch of love, hope and forgiveness will help you find positive solutions to the concerns weighing on your heart. As you study and share His Word, the Holy Spirit will lead you to grow in spiritual maturity and deeper faith experiences, and even reach out to those who face similar needs and concerns.

Four to five sessions each

Living with **Chronic Pain**
Suffering from **Guilt**
Living with **Change**
Coping with **Compassion Fatigue**

Living with **Compulsive Behaviors**
Discovering **Life after Divorce**
Living with **Infertility**
Surviving **Sexual Abuse**

3558 SOUTH JEFFERSON AVENUE
SAINT LOUIS, MISSOURI 63118-3968

© CPH 1994   H54920/2

Real lives facing real frustrations need Connections to God and to one another.

The **Connections** Bible study series helps take the concerns of your heart and turn them over to Jesus in worship, prayer, Bible study and discussion.

Connections uses a Gospel-centered message to build trust in God and to develop trusting and supportive relationships with one another, just as Christ intended.

Connections studies look at small portions of Scripture that really hit home, in areas where anxiety is often deepest.

For small groups or individual study, **Connections** uses God's Word to build relationships and bring peace to troubled hearts.

Ask for **Connections** at your Christian bookstore or call CPH, 1 800 325 3040

H54821

3558 SOUTH JEFFERSON AVENUE
SAINT LOUIS MISSOURI 63118-3968

Hear His Voice in . . .

God's Word for Today

This series helps you hear God speaking to you today — lovingly, emphatically, personally. As you study His Word book by book, you'll find: chapter-by-chapter background information; questions and learning experiences that promote exciting and challenging discussions; and activities that reveal how God speaks to the deepest concerns of your heart.

Each eight to 13 sessions

Amos: *And Justice for All*
Revelation: *Interpreting the Prophecy*
Psalms: *Conversations with God*
Genesis: *Rooted in Relationship*
Matthew: *His Kingdom Forever*
Galatians: *The Cost of Freedom*
1 Peter: *Claimed by God*
Colossians/Philemon: *Take a New Look at Christ*

3558 SOUTH JEFFERSON AVENUE
SAINT LOUIS, MISSOURI 63118-3968

© CPH 1994 H54920/1